POSTCARD HISTORY SERIES

Lighthouses of the Pacific Coast

NATIONAL LIGHTHOUSE DAY. In 1789, Congress passed an act for the establishment and support of lighthouses, beacons, buoys, and public piers. Two hundred years later, Congress passed a resolution designating August 7, 1989, as National Lighthouse Day. Here, Cape Argo, also known as the Cape Gregory Lighthouse, is pictured just south of the entrance to Coos Bay, Oregon. When first built in 1864, it was a 25-foot octagonal tower on a concrete foundation. (Author's collection.)

ON THE FRONT COVER: YAQUINA LIGHTHOUSE NEAR NEWPORT, OREGON. Construction began in 1871 and endured many delays because of the Oregon winters. The 93-foot-tall tower is the tallest lighthouse on the Oregon coast. (Author's collection.)

ON THE BACK COVER: POINT HUENEME LIGHTHOUSE, POINT HUENEME, CALIFORNIA. The light was built in 1873 in what was called a Craftsman style with Swiss and Elizabethan influences, as a two-story structure with a square tower that extended from the pitched roofline. (Author's collection.)

POSTCARD HISTORY SERIES

Lighthouses of the Pacific Coast

Linda Osborne Cynowa

ARCADIA
PUBLISHING

Published by Arcadia Publishing
Charleston, South Carolina

Printed in the United States of America

Library of Congress Control Number: 2024933549

For all general information contact Arcadia Publishing at:
Telephone 843-853-2070
Fax 843-853-0044
E-mail sales@arcadiapublishing.com

Visit us on the Internet at www.arcadiapublishing.com

This book is dedicated to all the historians and archivists who work so hard to keep the many pieces of our past safe for future generations.

To the lighthouse keepers, both men and women, who maintained the lights in the lonely conditions and helped to keep the lakes and seas as safe as possible for maritime navigation.

Contents

Acknowledgments   6

Introduction   7

1.   Alaska   9

2.   Washington   23

3.   Oregon   47

4.   California   67

5.   Hawaii   117

Bibliography   127

Acknowledgments

I would like to thank the many places where information on these important lighthouses can be obtained: Gastineau Channel Historical Society, Eldred Rock Lighthouse Preservation Society, Cape Decision Lighthouse Society, Juneau Lighthouse Society, Five Fingers Lighthouse Society, Keepers of the North Head Lighthouse, Keepers of Admiralty Head Lighthouse, Alki Point Lighthouse, Lime Kiln Lighthouse, West Point Lighthouse, Ediz Hook Lighthouse, Cape Disappointment Lighthouse, Semiahmoo Lighthouse, Cape Flattery Lighthouse, Point Wilson Lighthouse, Mukilteo Lighthouse, Turn Point Preservation Society, Westport-South Beach Historical Society, Friends of Yaquina Head Lighthouse, Friends of Point No Point, Friends of Cape Meares, Coquille River Lighthouse (Bullards Beach State Park), Friends of the Yaquina Bay Lighthouse, Inc., Cape Blanco Lighthouse, Cape Arago Lighthouse, Umpqua River Lighthouse, Old Point Loma Lighthouse, Point San Luis Lighthouse Keepers, St. George Reef Lighthouse Preservation Society, Point Cabrillo Light Keepers Association, Point Cabrillo Light Station, Point Pinos Lighthouse, Point Hueneme Lighthouse, Piedras Blancas Light Station, Alcatraz Island Light Station, Battery Point Lighthouse/Crescent City Lighthouse, Santa Cruz Lighthouse, The Mark Abbott Memorial Lighthouse/Santa Cruz Surfing Museum, Point Sur Light Station, Point Vincente Lighthouse, Point Bonita Lighthouse, Point Reys Lighthouse, Point Reyes Lighthouse, Trinity Head Lighthouse, Yerba Buena Island Lighthouse, New Point Loma Lighthouse, East Brother Lighthouse, Oakland Harbor Lighthouse, Pigeon Point Lighthouse, Point Arguello Lighthouse, Point Fermin Lighthouse Society, Aloha Tower Lighthouse, Diamond Head Lighthouse, Makapu'u Lighthouse, and Kilauea Lighthouse.

A grateful thank-you to the US Department of Homeland Security and the US Coast Guard Auxiliary, Phil Dougherty (Semiahmoo Lighthouse), US Lighthouse Society, William S. Hanable (Cape Flattery Lighthouse), *Lighthouse Digest* magazine, Bob King (Grave Point Light), the hitachiota collection (Diamond Head), and Valdez Museum & Historical Archive.

For further information on these important beacons of navigation, look into the many well-written and informative books by Jeremy D'Entremont.

It is with the greatest appreciation that I thank Julie Oparka, a certified archivist and historian, for her research abilities, editing, and very importantly, her photographic and technical support.

All postcards used, unless otherwise credited, are the property of the author. You can contact the author through the website lindaosbornecynowa.com for more information.

INTRODUCTION

As I previously mentioned in *Lighthouse of the Great Lakes* and *Lighthouses of the North Atlantic Coast*, lighthouses are towers or structures used to display a light for guiding maritime shipping. They are used to help guide and avoid dangerous areas, shoals, and reefs or just to find a safe harbor. The height of the tower and the intensity of the light will determine the distance the light can be seen out to sea. The lighthouse can be used, by how it is painted, to distinguish it from other lights in the area, this being called its daymark. During times when the sea and wind become at the most violent, the lighthouses provide early warnings of dangerous obstacles, such as submerged rocks, unseen cliffs, and even sandbars.

Its importance is that the brighter the light and the greater its height above the sea, the farther it can be seen to make navigation as safe as possible. This is much the same whether the lighthouse is on the Pacific coast, the Great Lakes, or the Atlantic coast, and their main objective has always been the same. On August 7, 1789, the federal government established the US Lighthouse Service, giving it responsibility for all aids to navigation and lighthouses. US Revenue Cutter Service, established in 1790 by Alexander Hamilton, the first secretary of the US Department of the Treasury, was formed to stop the loss of badly needed revenue by seagoing smugglers. Congress, realizing that aids to navigation were essential to maritime trade and the development of the West, authorized the establishment of lighthouses along the Pacific coast in 1848. The problem at the time was most of the Pacific coastline had not been explored. The federal government decided that an exploratory survey be undertaken to find the most advantageous sites to build these lighthouses. It was not until 1849 that this survey was conducted. In 1852, Congress created a nine-member lighthouse board to oversee all the operations and improve and revise where needed the entire system. Congress authorized the first group of lights in California at Fort Point, Fort Bonita, Alcatraz Island, Point Pinos, Point Lorna, Santa Barbara, Point Conception, the Farallon Islands, Humboldt Harbor, and Crescent City. Between 1852 and 1858, sixteen lights were erected in what today is California, Oregon, and Washington. Floating lightships were of very important use as in the case of the *Golden Gate*; the 110-foot cutter was built in Seattle in 1896 and arrived in San Francisco on May 13, 1897. The *Golden Gate* performed law enforcement boardings and towing and helped fumigate vessels in the Bay Area. One of her most unusual duties came during the great San Francisco earthquake of 1906. A great deal of the city's destruction was caused by fires. The men who served on the *Golden Gate* cutter served as firefighters and transported officials and refugees. Then, in the middle of their work, the commanding officer of the cutter was given the added responsibility of taking on board the gold reserve from the Federal Bank in San Francisco. The cutter remained a floating bank until the fire danger was over. On January 15, 1915, Congress created the US Coast Guard by merging the US Revenue Cutter Service and the US Life-Saving Service. This went on to have a great impact on lighthouses all over the country.

Dear Brother August:- Your letter rec'd very glad to hear from you, hope you will soon send the next one your sister. With best wishes, I am as ever, Agnes.

Point Loma Lighthouse, San Diego, Cal.

THE POSTAL ACT. The Postal Act of May 19, 1898, provided for the extensive private product of postcards to measure 3.25 by 5.5 inches. Messages could only be written on the front. The back was reserved "exclusively for the address." After March 1, 1907, the law specified that messages could be written on the backs of cards. Cards of this new style were "divided back" because of the vertical line, to the left of which the message could be written, with the address on the right. Undivided back cards remained in the inventories of shops for many years.

One

ALASKA

GRAVEYARD POINT LIGHT, BRISTOL BAY. The Federal Light House Service, as it was called before the establishment of the US Coast Guard, had navigational lights as well as lighthouses. This light was a navigational light intended to help ships get to their canneries based upriver. The Kvichak River is one of five of the leading producers of sockeye salmon in Bristol Bay with annual catches in the tens of millions. Canneries were built on many rivers, including the "Graveyard Cannery" near the entrance to the Kvichak, also called the Koggiung. The light was probably refueled by nearby cannery crews during the summer and ignored the rest of the year. The cannery closed in 1957.

Princess May wrecked on Sentinel Island, Alaska - August 5th, 1910

SENTINEL ISLAND LIGHTHOUSE, JUNEAU. On August 5, 1910, the *Princess May* departed Skagway, Alaska, with 80 passengers, 68 crew, and a shipment of gold. The ship was steaming down the Lynn Canal at 12 knots under heavy fog in the command of Capt. John McLeo when it stuck the rocks near the north end of Sentinel Island early in the morning. It was high tide, and the momentum of the ship forced it well up onto the rocks, with the bow jutting upward at an angle of 23 degrees. No lives were lost, thanks to the Sentinel Island Lighthouse keeper's help.

B. Wreck of "Princess May" Sentinel Is. Alaska. Aug. 6th 1910.   KINTER & POND.

ADDITIONAL VIEWS OF SENTINEL ISLAND LIGHTHOUSE. In 1902, a lighthouse was built 25 miles northwest of Juneau on the east side of the Lynn Canal, with a square wooden tower attached to the front western side of the two-story keepers' duplex with cross gables. A lantern room housing a fourth-order Fresnel lens had a range of 14 miles. A 360-foot tram was built of steel rails with wooden ties to connect the dock and boathouse with the lighthouse. By 1935, a need for a new lighthouse saw a concrete Art Deco–style building constructed. The lantern room was slid on a trestle from the old tower onto the new 51-foot tower. The original lighthouse without the tower was kept in use to house additional keepers until the station was automated in 1966. The original dwelling was demolished in 1971.

MARY ISLAND LIGHTHOUSE, KETCHIKAN. In 1903, the new Mary Island Lighthouse was established 25 miles south of Ketchikan. For those sailing from Canada to the Alaskan Territory, a customhouse was established on the island. As with its neighbor Tree Point Light, Mary Island Light was an octagonal, one-story building with a tower extending from the center of the building, 50 feet high. The lantern room held a fourth-order Fresnel lens. By 1938, a reinforced concrete Art Deco–style light was constructed with a square tower attached to the flat roof of the one-story building. Two dwellings were added behind the station to house the lightkeepers and their families. The US Coast Guard personnel were removed from the lighthouse when it was automated in 1969. The Fresnel lens is now part of a display at the Juneau-Douglas Museum.

CAPE DECISION LIGHTHOUSE, KUIU ISLAND. In 1925, the US Lighthouse Service suggested that Cape Decision Point should have a lighthouse constructed there, as the locality had shown to be dangerous for navigation in foggy weather because of the strong tidal currents, the jagged shoreline, and many rocks just offshore. By 1932, a reinforced concrete lighthouse with a dock and tramway, derrick and hoisting machinery, a boathouse, and helicopter pad had been constructed and activated on Cape Decision. The concrete lighthouse was a one-story square building with a central square tower, 75 feet tall, holding a third-order Fresnel lens. This light was the first lighthouse in the Alaska Territory to use electricity. In 1989, the keeper was burning trash and it caught fire, lighting the pier. Luckily, the fire was extinguished before it reached the lighthouse. (Both, courtesy of the US Coast Guard Collection.)

Boat returning from Landing the Mail at Cape Sarichef Lighthouse, Alaska.
Mail is received four or five times yearly.   This station is described as the most-out-of-the-way place in the world."

POINT SARICHEF LIGHTHOUSE, UNIMAK ISLAND. The lighthouse sits on the northwestern corner of Unimak Island, one of the Aleutian Islands, where the entrance opens to the Bering Sea. In 1904, an octagonal wood building with a wooden tower 45 feet in height, housing the third-order Fresnel lens, was constructed. By later that first year, storms had damaged the lighthouse, boathouse, enginehouse, and derrick near the reef that needed replacing. Because of the tsunami that washed away the neighboring light at Scotch Cap just 20 miles away in 1946, the lighthouse was rebuilt. Because of the extreme isolation of the light station, the lightkeepers were stationed there for only one year at a time. In 1979, the lighthouse became automated when a steel skeleton and light beacon were used to replace the light. The lighthouse was demolished in 1999.

CAPE SARICHEF LIGHT, ALASKA   U.S. COAST GUARD PHOTO

POINT SHERMAN LIGHTHOUSE, LYNN CANAL. Located 38 miles north of Juneau, Point Sherman Lighthouse was built in 1904 as a one-and-a-half-story keeper's dwelling with a black hexagon lantern room and a white-painted hexagon tower just six feet in height. Its original optics was an acetylene lantern. By 1917, the lighthouse was automated, and the keepers were removed.

GUARD ISLAND LIGHTHOUSE, TONGASS NARROWS. Of the two rocky isles at the northern entrance to the Tongass Narrows, Guard Island, being the largest of the two, held the lighthouse built in 1904. A 34-foot-tall square pyramidal wooden tower held the lantern with a Fresnel lens that gave a fixed white light. A two-story keeper's house was built, along with a boathouse and oil storage house. By the early 1960s, the outbuildings and lighthouse were demolished.

POINT RETREAT LIGHTHOUSE, ADMIRALTY ISLAND. The light station had a six-foot-tall wooden hexagonal-shaped tower with a lantern room and was situated on the Mansfield Peninsula in what was the Alaska Territory in 1904. In 1924, after the light had been downgraded 10 years before to a minor light, two new keepers' dwellings, a boathouse, and a landing wharf were added to the station. This new light was lit with an acetylene light. That same year, one of the two dwellings burned to the ground, and soon, a replacement residence was needed. In 1966, one of the keepers' homes was removed for a helicopter pad, and soon after, in 1973, the lighthouse was downgraded to a minor light once again, and all persons were removed. The Alaska Lighthouse Society took over ownership in 1997. A new lantern room was placed on the tower in 2004.

SCOTCH CAP LIGHTHOUSE, UNIMAK ISLAND, IN THE ALEUTIANS. The year 1903 saw the first Scotch Cap Lighthouse built as an octagonal wood-constructed structure with a 45-foot light tower. A fog signal building and two oil houses were soon added to the station. At the most westerly point of the Alaskan mainland, it was found to be one of the foggiest places in the world. By 1940, a new concrete lighthouse was built to replace the wood-constructed structure. During the early morning hours of April 1, 1946, a 100-foot-tall tsunami propelled by a 7.4-magnitude earthquake under the northern Pacific came ashore at Scotch Cap, crushing the lighthouse and killing the five-man crew. The lighthouse keepers of Scotch Cap who died in the tsunami were Anthony Petit, the lighthouse keeper, and Coastguardsmen Leonard Pickering, machinist mate; Jack Colvin, fireman; Dewey Dykstra, seaman; and Paul Ness, seaman. The new lighthouse was constructed on higher ground. Keepers depicted in the card below in 1910 are Sigvart G. Olsen on the left and Michael Ludescher on the right.

ELDRED ROCK, LYNN CANAL, ALASKA   746 LNP

ELDRED ROCK LIGHTHOUSE, LYNN CANAL. In the stormy waters of the Lynn Canal sits a small island surrounded by snow-covered mountains. Eldred Rock was to be the last of 12 lighthouses built in Alaskan territory between 1902 and 1906, an octagonal concrete two-story building with an octagonal wood tower protruding from the center of the roof line. The light tower was situated 91 feet above sea level, giving it a 15-mile visibility. The light station was on 2.4 acres and contained a wooden boathouse, a tramway, and a carpenter shop. A third-order Fresnel lens was housed in the lantern room of the 56-foot lighthouse tower.

ELDRED ROCK LIGHT HOUSE

ADDITIONAL VIEWS OF ELDRED ROCK LIGHTHOUSE. In 1966, a helicopter pad was built on the northern end of the island for bringing supplies to the station. By 1973, the personnel of Eldred Rock was removed, along with the fog signal and radio beacon, when the light then became automated. After the light was automated, the US Coast Guard no longer used the lighthouse for any other purpose other than for aid to navigation. In 1975, Eldred Rock Lighthouse was entered into the National Register of Historic Places, where it became a subject of the Department of the Interior Standards of Rehabilitation.

FIVE FINGER ISLANDS LIGHTHOUSE, FREDERICK SOUND. A collection of what looks like "boney fingers" comprises the Five Finger Islands, with some of those rocky protrusions only appearing at low tide. It is located between the Stephens Passage and Frederick Sound in the southeastern portion of Alaska. In 1902, this first light was a two-story, rectangular building with a square tower, raised from the hipped roof line with a fourth-order Fresnel lens in the lantern room, showing a fixed white light. In 1933, a fire started, after some repair work being done, and with the frozen pipes, the lighthouse soon was a total loss. In 1935, a concrete Art Deco–style 40-foot-square light was newly established on the island, with enough room to house three keepers. In 1984, the last US Coast Guard crew left the island, and it become an unmanned light. (Below, courtesy of the US Coast Guard Collection.)

TREE POINT LIGHTHOUSE, REVILLAGIGEDO CHANNEL. The year 1903 saw the first of two lighthouses built at Tree Point, just seven miles north of the Canadian border. A total of 680 acres were used for the Tree Point Light Station. This lighthouse was the only light built on the mainland of Alaska. By 1935, the government felt that the use of reinforced concrete would have better benefit in the harsh terrain, and work was started on the second light at Tree Point in the Art Deco style, with poured concrete used for the 18-by-36-foot building with a 13-foot-square tower with a height of 58 feet. The fourth-order lens from the old light was transferred to the new light by 1935. The light station had three wood-frame dwellings placed behind the light tower, along with a small school building. The light was automated in 1969. (Both, courtesy of the US Coast Guard Collection.)

CAPE HINCHINBROOK LIGHTHOUSE, PRINCE WILLIAM SOUND. Cape Hinchinbrook Lighthouse served as a beacon to mark the entrance to Prince William Sound and to warn of the dangerous shallows. Constructed in 1906, it took four years to build. In 1920, an earthquake struck the area. The damage sustained required the original hexagonal light to be replaced with a 67-foot-tall Art Deco concrete structure that was completed in 1934. By 1967, the Fresnel lens was replaced by an aero beacon, with full automation to take place in 1974. The US Coast Guard transferred ownership of the light to the State of Alaska in 1975. (Courtesy of the US Coast Guard Collection.)

Two

WASHINGTON

A TALE OF TWO LIGHTS. At the mouth of the Columbia River channel, mariners found that the Cape Disappointment Lighthouse was often obscured when approaching the river. Concern was great because of the many shipwrecks along the peninsula. In 1898, the light was first lit with a fixed-white light, while the Cape Disappointment Light, just two miles north, used an alternating light of red and white flashes. The new lighthouse on Cape Disappointment was called North Head Lighthouse.

NORTH HEAD LIGHTHOUSE, ILWACO.
The light was constructed of brick on a sandstone foundation, then using a cement plaster overlay. A 65-foot tower with a lantern room and a first-order Fresnel lens was brought from Cape Disappointment. Soon, a keeper's residence, two oil houses, a barn, and duplex housing for the assistant keepers rounded out the light station. Being a lightkeeper at North Head Light meant getting used to a very remote and hard life. It helped when there were three keepers in residence to have work schedules of eight hours a shift. Usually, one keeper worked from dusk until dawn, and others did the maintenance during the daylight hours to keep it in top working order.

North Head Lighthouse, Washington.

ADDITIONAL VIEWS OF NORTH HEAD LIGHTHOUSE. In 1937, the first-order lens was changed to a fourth-order lens. By this time, electricity has been brought to the light station. With this being one of the windiest spots in the United States, for a short time, a US Weather Bureau was built at the station but eventually closed by 1955. The light was automated in 1961, and at that time, the last lightkeeper left. The lighthouse was transferred to the Keepers of North Head Lighthouse group in 2012 for restoration purposes. North Head has remained a light station with all its original buildings intact.

NORTH HEAD LIGHT
LONG BEACH, WASH.

RED BLUFF AND ADMIRALTY HEAD LIGHTHOUSE, WHIDBEY ISLAND. The Red Bluff Lighthouse was a wooden two-story schoolhouse style with a light tower rising from the pitched roof. Painted white when it was built and operational in 1861, the lantern room housed a fourth-order Fresnel lens. This was the first of two lighthouses at Admiralty Head. When the new Fort Casey was constructed in 1897, this light was moved to give space for gun batteries on the bluff. After the new Admiralty Head Lighthouse was finished, the old light was used to house the Coastal Artillery Army for a number of years. The original Red Bluff was demolished in 1928.

Fort Casey Light-House, Wash.

ADDITIONAL VIEWS OF ADMIRALTY HEAD LIGHTHOUSE. The first keeper at the new light was Capt. Charles Davis and his wife, Delia Overton Davis. This second Admiralty Head Lighthouse was a two-story dwelling, with three bedrooms on the second floor, a kitchen, living room, and dining area downstairs, and an indoor bathroom, with access to the tower was through the dwelling's foyer. Using brick then covered in stucco, it was built in a Spanish style. In 1928, the lighthouse was deactivated, and the lantern was removed. The US Army used the lighthouse during World War II after painting it an olive green. Washington State Parks restored the light with help from the Washington State University Extension Office.

ALKI POINT LIGHTHOUSE, WEST SEATTLE. Alki Point is at the southernmost entrance to Elliott Bay at Puget Sound. The land was sold to Hans Martin Hanson in 1868. Farmer Hanson hung a brass kerosene lantern from a post attached to the side of his barn because of the dangerous shoals. In 1887, a post lantern was used to replace the farmer's lantern and placed on the point until a permanent lighthouse could be built. Originally, a kerosene and acetylene lamp was used to provide illumination. Because the point belonged to Hans Hanson, he was paid $15 a month to light and extinguish the light, along with cleaning the glass, overseeing the fuel, and trimming the wick, thus becoming the first official lightkeeper at Alki Point. In 1900, the point went to his son, who kept it lit for another 10 years.

ALKI LIGHTHOUSE AND OLYMPIC MOUNTAINS · SEATTLE · WA 1012

ADDITIONAL VIEWS OF ALKI POINT LIGHTHOUSE. In 1913, because of the shoals and reefs and what would make a good harbor light, a 37-foot octagonal, concrete tower with an attached building for the fog signal was constructed on Alki Point. During that time, two homes were also built behind the light to house the lighthouse keepers and their families. The tower held a fourth-order Fresnel lens with a visibility of 12 miles. The last lighthouse keeper, Albert Anderson, left the light in 1970. Until the 1980s, the operating principles at Alki Point were manually used. Coastguardsmen were responsible for turning the light on at dusk and off at daybreak. In 1984, the light became fully automated. Today, the lighthouse is monitored by the US Coast Guard.

THE ALKI POINT LIGHTHOUSE, SEATTLE, U.S.A.

EDIZ HOOK LIGHTHOUSE, PORT ANGELES. In Port Angeles, the Northwest's deepest harbor, a three-and-a-half-mile long sand spit, an accumulation of sand usually attached to land at one end, is the area called Ediz Hook. President Lincoln, in 1862, signed an order that the end of the spit be used for governmental purposes. In 1865, the original two-story schoolhouse-design lighthouse was constructed with a square tower at the end of the pitched roof. In 1885, a 15-foot fog bell tower was built with a one-and-a-half-ton bell that hung from the top beams of the structure. Using a clock mechanism, every 15 seconds during foggy weather the bell would ring. The years saw changes to the fog bell to make the sound more effective. By the time of the new century, a new light was needed.

ADDITIONAL VIEWS OF EDIZ HOOK LIGHTHOUSE. In 1908, a new fog signal building with an attached octagonal light tower and a separate keeper's dwelling was constructed at the station. The fifth-order Fresnel lens was removed from the old tower and placed in the new tower. A beacon was used to replace the second lighthouse, placed at a US Coast Guard air station in 1946. The 1908 lighthouse became a private dwelling after being removed from the station area. The original 1865 light was demolished in 1939. This second lighthouse was destined to last only about 40 years, when it was replaced by a modern beacon at the Coast Guard station in Port Angeles. The 1908 light was sold for use as a private residence after being removed by barge across the harbor.

CAPE DISAPPOINTMENT LIGHT HOUSE

VINCENT'S SOUVENIR STORE LONG BEACH

CAPE DISAPPOINTMENT LIGHTHOUSE

CAPE DISAPPOINTMENT, ILWACO. At the mouth of the Columbia River sits Cape Disappointment, and because of the force of the river, it is one of the most dangerous marine areas with many ships meeting a sad end. A prominent cape on the north side of the river made this a good stop for a light. It was soon found that ships arriving from the north had very little visibility. This was rectified by building the lighthouse at North Head two miles away. North Head received the first-order lens that had been ordered for Cape Disappointment, and it had a fifth-order lens installed. Most lighthouses had the tower and dwellings connected, but at Farallon Island and Cape Disappointment, the keepers' dwellings had to be located a quarter mile away.

ADDITIONAL VIEWS OF CAPE DISAPPOINTMENT. The tower at Cape Disappointment was built in 1856 of brick and stands 53 feet tall with a diameter at the base of 14 feet around and 10 feet at the top lantern room. A duplex with 11 rooms on each side was built, with one side for the head keeper and the two assistants sharing the other side. In 1871, a full light station was established at the cape. In 1936, a radio beacon was installed, and the next year, the light was electrified. Although the US Coast Guard wanted to close the light down in 1956, the Columbia River pilots had concerns. Cape Disappointment was fully automated in 1973 and is still active today.

5159 U. S. LIGHTHOUSE BLAINE WASH.

SEMIAHMOO HARBOR LIGHTHOUSE, BLAINE. The Semiahmoo Lighthouse was constructed in 1905 using the same plans as Drayton Harbor Light. It was a octagonal-shaped 62-by-28-foot Victorian-style building on a platform in Semiahmoo Bay at the entrance to Drayton Harbor near Blaine. That platform measured 50 by 80 feet with 117 piles driven 15 feet into the sand bank and was painted white with a light green trim and a bronze-colored roof. An automated light was added to the site, but the structure was demolished in 1944.

LIGHTHOUSE AT BLAINE

Willapan Harbor Lighthouse No 13

WILLAPA BAY HARBOR, CAPE SHOALWATER. From the very start in 1858, there were issues at Willapa Bay Lighthouse. Built in the Cape Cod style with its tower and lantern room resting on the simple cottage, the light was soon closed because of the challenge of getting fuel for the light. Relit in 1861, erosion and sifting sand were continual issues for the light. Demolition was necessary by 1940 when the west wall slid into the ocean.

NEW DUNGENESS LIGHTHOUSE, SEQUIM. The original lighthouse was a one-and-a-half-story sandstone and brick duplex with a 92-foot tower with a red lantern room rising from the pitched roof. In 1927, thirty feet were removed from the height of the tower due to long remaining cracks that appeared after an earthquake hit the area in 1861. It also received a new, smaller lantern room at the same time.

Cape Flattery Lighthouse, Washington.

CAPE FLATTERY, NEAH BAY. A lighthouse was built on Tatoosh Island in 1857, in the northwestern point of the United States, as a navigational aid to mariners entering the Strait of Juan de Fuca. Because of thick fog and especially the strong currents, ships could be carried toward the dangerous shores of Vancouver Island. Placing the light on Tatoosh Island allowed marine shipping to enter the strait at night. Tatoosh Island is a 20-acre rock ledge lying one-half mile off Cape Flattery. Because of its height from the water being 100 feet, landing ships for restocking was a hazardous undertaking.

Tatoosh Island

ADDITIONAL VIEWS OF CAPE FLATTERY. A one-and-a-half-story Cape Cod–style sandstone dwelling was built with two-foot-thick walls. The main floor consisted of the dining, kitchen, and living rooms. Four bedrooms were in the upper story. A 65-foot brick lighthouse tower was constructed in the center of the building. The first-order Fresnel lens had a fixed white light with a visibility of 20 miles. In 1883, the telegraph was brought to the island by the longest cable hung, which stretched from the island to the mainland. In 1904, that cable went underground. The year 1932 had the first-order lens being downgraded to a fourth-order. By 1977, the lighthouse was automated.

POINT WILSON LIGHTHOUSE, PORT TOWNSEND. The first lighthouse built at the entrance to Admiralty Inlet in 1879, was a two-story Cape Cod–style dwelling with a wooden, square-shaped tower attached to the roof. The lantern room held a fourth-order Fresnel lens with a visibility of 13 miles. Because of the high water and storms in the area, the sandy beach continued to erode, and even with the help of fencing, by 1904 stones used as reinforcement were put in place, but threats to the lighthouse continued. By 1914, a new light was built to replace the first. The new lighthouse was built of concrete with a 49-foot octagon-shaped tower and the original fourth-order lens.

Point Wilson Lighthouse. - Near Port Townsend.

ADDITIONAL VIEWS OF POINT WILSON LIGHTHOUSE. The original lighthouse without the tower attached served as additional living quarters for keepers. At 51 feet above the water, the lens is the highest of all the lighthouses on Puget Sound. When World War II began, Point Wilson, along with other lights, were extinguished to give safety to the nearby Fort Worden. The light became automated in 1976, with the US Coast Guard occupying the light until 2000. Although erosion to the land around the light still continues, the US Lighthouse Society leased the lighthouse from the Coast Guard in 2019.

POINT NO POINT LIGHTHOUSE, HANSVILLE. One and a half miles from Hansville in the northeastern point of Kitsap County sits a sandy bar that extends a quarter mile into the water, at the entrance to Puget Sound. In 1879, an 11-foot square tower with a fixed, fifth-order Fresnel lens and a keepers' duplex was built; soon, a brick-built watch room was added to the station. For the first few years, supplies were brought in by boat. In 1880, a four-mile trail was established through the dense ground to receive mail and supplies from Port Gamble. The station was automated in 1977. The US Lighthouse Society uses part of the keepers' duplex as an office for its lighthouse research library. (Above, courtesy of the US Coast Guard Collection.)

LIME KILN LIGHTHOUSE, SAN JUAN ISLAND. The lighthouse sits at the entrance to Haro Strait, which links Puget Sound and the Strip of Georgia, a major shipping channel. In 1919, a concrete fog signal building was constructed with a 38-foot octagonal tower holding a fourth-order Fresnel lens attached. Two concrete keepers' houses were built with bathrooms and basements and were large enough for the families to reside. The light station was fully automated by 1962.

WEST POINT LIGHTHOUSE, SEATTLE. Situated at the end of a long sandy point that extends into Puget Sound, in 1881, an 11-foot square brick tower, with an attached octagonal lantern room housing the fourth-order Fresnel lens and oil room, was constructed. A one-and-a-half-story frame cottage with five rooms was built for the keeper and his family. It was automated in 1985. (Courtesy of the US Coast Guard Collection.)

MUKILTEO LIGHTHOUSE, MUKILTEO.
While usual for the time, the wood-frame Colonial Revival–style octagonal 38-foot tower was not built of brick or concrete used on other lights. It started out with a fourth-order revolving Fresnel lens. It was constructed as a combination fog signal building and tower with a separate keeper's house at the station. With the onset of electricity in 1927, a fixed fourth-order lens was installed. Ownership went to the City of Mukilteo in 2001.

LIGHT HOUSE ~ MUKILTEO · WASH.

TURN POINT LIGHTHOUSE, STUART ISLAND. Overlooking the Haro Strait on the western end of Stuart Island, a turn is made in the shipping lanes between Haro and Boundary Pass. This is where, in 1893, a light station with a duplex keepers' dwelling, fog signal building, water tanks, barns, and boathouse were to be constructed. The light station was electrified in 1925, becoming automated in 1975. It is still in use for navigation today.

Grays Harbor Light
Westport Washington

THE WESTPORT LIGHT. Located on the south side of the entrance to Grays Harbor is the entryway to the Straits of Juan de Fuca. Westport had a large number of lumber, logging, and shipyards near the port in the late 1800s. A first-order light was soon realized as a necessity to the harbor. It took time to obtain the property needed for the light on a parcel of land at Point Chehalis, on the southern side of Grays Harbor. With the owners of the parcel not willing to sell until proceedings were initiated, the court agreed upon a fair price. A cornerstone was laid for the lighthouse on August 23, 1897.

B. 2042. U. S. Lighthouse at Westport, near Aberdeen, Wash.

GRAYS HARBOR (WESTPORT) LIGHTHOUSE, WESTPORT. The tower, at 107 feet tall, became the tallest lighthouse in Washington and the third tallest along the Pacific coast. In 1897, the Late Victorian Italianate–style lighthouse was built with a tower having walls four feet thick near the base, using brick and then coated in concrete on the exterior walls. It took 137 steps to reach the top. The windows originally used for light were eventually cemented over because of the cost of maintenance. At the time when the tower was built, on a 12-foot thick layer of sandstone, two keepers' dwellings, one a single residence and the other a duplex for the assistant keepers; an oil house; a fog signal building; and windmill were constructed. A third-order Fresnel lens was used with both white and red sequences of flashes.

WESTPORT LIGHT HOUSE

ANOTHER VIEW OF GRAYS HARBOR LIGHTHOUSE. In 1992, although the lantern room still had the original Fresnel lens, it had been turned off for use of a smaller light that has been mounted in the lantern-room balcony with a 35-watt light bulb still offering a visibility of 19 miles. By 1998, a lease agreement was signed between the US Coast Guard and the Westport-South Beach Historical Society. The society was granted ownership of the lighthouse in 2004 when restoration plans were put into place and the light opened up to the public, where it adjoins the Westport State Park.

Three

OREGON

YAQUINA LIGHT HOUSE NEAR NEWPORT, OREGON. CAV-17

THE CAPE FOULWEATHER LIGHT. Usually referred to as Cape Foulweather, due to the mariners dealing with foul weather when near its position, it was not until the 1890s before the name Yaquina Head was used to refer to the light. The lighthouse is located near the mouth of the Yaquina River near Newport at Yaquina Head. Construction began in 1871 and endured many delays because of the Oregon winters. Landing building materials was made difficult when supplies were taken instead to Newport and then carted six miles back to the site over more difficult roads.

YAQUINA HEAD LIGHTHOUSE, NEWPORT.
The 93-foot-tall tower is the tallest
lighthouse tower on the Oregon coast and
was built with bricks from a California
brick company. It has been said that over
370,000 bricks were used to complete
the project. They used a double wall
when building the tower to keep out the
dampness and make it more insulated. The
tower light shines 162 feet above the water
and has a visibility of 19 miles with its first-
order Fresnel lens by Barbier & Fenestre.
By 1872, the keepers' residence was built as
a two-story duplex, with the keeper residing
on one side and the assistant keepers
sharing the other side. Maintenance and
storage buildings were added as needed for
use with the three lightkeepers on duty. By
1920, additional housing was built at the
light station.

#218 Lighthouse, Newport

ADDITIONAL VIEWS OF YAQUINA HEAD LIGHTHOUSE. Lighthouses, by the nature of things, are usually put in airy exposed areas, which makes dealing with the storms, water, and nature, in general, a difficult time for the lighthouses and their keepers. Usually sitting high upon cliffs, the wind and water will work against the cliffs and create erosion that becomes unhealthy for the light's stability. Electricity was brought to the station by 1933. The original keepers' duplex was torn down in 1938 and replaced by a smaller residence. The US Coast Guard left the station when the light became automated in 1966. Many of the unused buildings were demolished in 1984. By 1993, the Friends of Yaquina Lighthouse used interpretation in teaching visitors about the light and work toward the preservation of the tower.

YAQUINA HEAD LIGHTHOUSE - OREGON COAST

CAPE MEARES LIGHTHOUSE, TILLAMOOK COUNTY. It was originally called Cape Lookout by the explorer Capt. John Mears in 1788, but by the 1850s, it was realized the name on maps was being used by a light 10 miles to the south. In 1890, Cape Mears Lighthouse was built overlooking Tillamook Bay. The station had two one-and-a-half-story keepers' quarters with seven rooms each. These dwellings were located 1,000 feet up the hill from the tower itself. The head keepers used one house, and the assistants shared the other dwelling. Two brick cisterns were built to hold water from the spring. The 38-foot tower, built of bricks made on-site and then covered in iron sheeting, was the shortest lighthouse in Oregon and had a visibility of 21 miles because of its location and first-order Fresnel lens.

Cape Meares - Oregon Coast

Christian 471

ADDITIONAL VIEWS OF CAPE MEARES LIGHTHOUSE. When electricity came to the cape in 1934, there was no longer a use for the oil houses, and they were removed. A concrete block house was used when the light was decommissioned in 1963, and an automated beacon was installed. When local citizens complained about the removal of the old lighthouse, the property was then leased to Tillamook County. The keepers' dwellings were removed, and eventually, a parking lot was put in their place. But vandals soon completed the job that nature usually does when something is neglected. Today, the light is in the hands of the Friends of Cape Meares and the Cape Meares State Scenic Viewpoint.

Cape Meares Light House, Oregon Coast

1375. Lighthouse No 5 on the Oregon Coast.

COQUILLE RIVER LIGHTHOUSE, BRANDON. When first completed, it was originally called the Brando Light because of the shifting sanolars in the Coquills River, and with the Brannon Harbor having such a dangerous area for marine traffic, a light was soon necessary, and construction started in 1895. Before the light could be started, a leveling of the rocky ground was needed on Rockliff Rock, where stone was cut for the foundation. A cylindrical tower was attached to the octagonal signal equipment room on the east side of the building. A keepers' duplex, with three bedrooms, a dining room with a kitchen, and a sitting room, was attached to the tower by a wooden walkway, running 650 feet in length.

ADDITIONAL VIEWS OF COQUILLE RIVER LIGHTHOUSE. In 1936, an out-of-control forest fire swept into the town of Brandon and burned all but 16 of the town's many hundreds of buildings. With most of the town gone, shipping to the area declined. By 1939, at the south jetty, an automatic light was erected, and the Coquille River light was shut down. In 1939, the US Coast Guard felt the lighthouse was no longer needed. It was abandoned and soon in need of major repair. In 1976, a renovation took place to erase the damage done by vandals, and it was opened to the public in 1979. A new restoration project in 2007 to fix damaged stucco, roof tiles, and exterior painting was undertaken. The lighthouse is now part of Bullard's Beach State Park.

WILLAMETTE RIVER LIGHT, PORTLAND. The entrance to the Willamette River is very narrow where it connects to the Columbia River and foggy weather makes entering the channel challenging. In 1895, the newly built octagonal light station was put into service. In 1935, the Willamette River Light was deactivated. In the years since 1935, while being unattended, it caught fire and burned to the ground in the 1950s.

DESDEMONA SANDS LIGHTHOUSE, COLUMBIA BAR. A number of lighthouses marked the entrance to the Columbia River, with the Desdemona Sands in the south, a sandy islet that created a shoal that had dangerous issues for shipping. Built on top of straight wooden piles, the light was a one-and-a-half-story octagonal building. It was electrified in 1935, eliminating the need for a keeper from that point on. The building was demolished in 1942. The foundation was removed in 1964.

YAQUINA BAY LIGHTHOUSE, NEWPORT.
Land bought in 1871 from Lester and
Sophroni Baldwin of 36 acres had a price
of $500 in gold. The two-story clapboard
dwelling with an attached light tower was
located on the north side of the entrance
to Yaquina Bay. Its fifth-order Fresnel
lens only shone from November 1871
until October 1874 because of the larger
Yaquina Head Light built in 1873, located
four miles north. The light was empty for
14 years and soon fell into disrepair. In
1906, the US Life-Saving Service used the
dwelling to house a crew. In 1915, the US
Life-Saving Service formed the US Coast
Guard. The Coast Guard used the dwelling
until 1933. Friends of the Yaquina Bay
Lighthouse was formed in 1988, and along
with the Oregon State Parks Department,
the organization maintains the light today.

5. The Old Lighthouse, Newport, Oregon

68. USLS Station
Newport Ore.

TILLAMOOK ROCK LIGHTHOUSE, CLATSOP COUNTY. Located just over a mile from Tillamook Head in the Pacific Ocean and 20 miles south of the Columbia River, the lighthouse sits atop an acre of volcanic rock. At times, it was called "Terrible Tilly" because of the horrible weather conditions, isolation, and continuing environmental hazards for all that worked there. Supplies could be delayed for days or even weeks. Workers had to dynamite the rocks' rounded areas to flatten a portion to hold the lighthouse. Soon, a one-story stone dwelling was built at 48 by 45 feet with a 62-foot-tall tower and 32-by-28-foot lantern room with a first-order Fresnel lens. After working for 575 days for the building to take place, the light was first lit in January 1881.

TILLAMOOK ROCK AND LIGHTHOUSE, PORTLAND, OREGON.

5555. COPYRIGHT, 1901, BY DETROIT PHOTOGRAPHIC CO.

HALE 261. Tillamook Light - Oregon Coast

ADDITIONAL VIEWS OF TILLAMOOK ROCK LIGHTHOUSE. In the following year, on the northeast slope of the rock, a brick engine and supply house was built. A landing wharf was needed and attached to the keepers' dwellings along with a tramway to help raise supplies from the wharf to the supply house. There would always be continual repairs to be made to the light and surrounding buildings because of water and storm damage. Tillamook Rock Lighthouse was decommissioned in 1957, with a history of being the most expensive lighthouse to operate. It passed to private hands a number of times over the next few years. The light shone for 77 years because of the bravery of those lightkeepers who went to such lengths to keep that it burning.

Boyer 262. Tillamook Light near Seaside, Oregon

MOORER

C 13 628 - Cape Blanco Light House, Oregon Coast Highway.

CAPE BLANCO LIGHTHOUSE, CAPE BLANCO. On Oregon's southernmost coast, a mile and a half out into the ocean, a lighthouse was built in 1870 whose basic function was to warn approaching ships of the dangerous reefs. Roads to this area of the cape were nonexistent at the time. It was found that having the bricks needed for the tower and outbuildings would be best made on-site. On a foundation of concrete, a tower 50 feet tall held a first-order Fresnel lens with a visibility of 23 miles. At the time, an oil room was built to connect the two. A two-story brick duplex, containing seven rooms on each side, was built at a distance of 125 feet from the tower itself. As with most other lighthouses, the head keeper resided on one side while his assistants shared the other side.

ADDITIONAL VIEWS OF CAPE BLANCO LIGHTHOUSE. It was not until 1885 that a road was built leading up to the station for the delivery of supplies, which is now connected to the country road leading to the nearest landing at Port Orford. By 1910, a second, larger keeper's dwelling was added to the light station due to crowding from enlarging families. By 1980, the light was automated, and then all staff was removed. With an empty lighthouse, vandals damaged the lens, which cost $80,000 to repair. Over the years, the two keepers' dwellings and utility buildings, including the oil house, were removed. The tower still stands and accepts visitors today.

Cape Blanco Light House, Oregon Coast

Coos Head Light House, Oregon Coast Highway. 765.

CAPE ARAGO LIGHTHOUSE, CHARLESTON. When first built in 1864, just south of the entrance to Coos Bay, Cape Argo Lighthouse had a 25-foot octagonal tower on a concrete foundation with a skeleton base connecting a 1,300-foot wooden walkway attached to the keeper's house. A lifesaving station was established at the light in 1878, although it was reestablished on the mainland in 1891 because of better accessibility. By 1896, the tower was strengthened with bricks and a stucco covering, and a new duplex dwelling for the keepers was added to the site. Because of the inclement weather and erosion at most times of the year, a new light was built in 1909 with a 100-foot-tall tower.

CAPE ARAGO LIGHT, COOS BAY

ADDITIONAL VIEWS OF CAPE ARAGO LIGHTHOUSE. There were a number of lighthouses and towers at Cape Argo; the original lighthouse was blown up in 1936, the keepers' dwelling razed in 1957, and the second lighthouse demolished in the 1960s. After the US Coast Guard took over the light, the personnel lived on the mainland across from the lighthouse, up until the light was automated in 1966. The Fresnel lens was removed from the tower in 1993. The light was deactivated in 2006. In 2013, the government transferred the Cape Argo Lighthouse to the Confederated Tribes of the Coos, with the condition that the light be made available to the general public and used for historical preservation purposes.

15-405 Heceta Head Light House - O.C.H. 101

HECETA HEAD LIGHT, FLORENCE. In the 90 miles between the Cape Argo Light and Yaquina Head Light, along the Oregon coast at Heceta Head and the Umpqua River, 19 acres were used to build a lighthouse with a first-order Fresnel lens in 1892. The brick tower is 56 feet tall and has a focal plane of 205 feet above sea level, with a visibility of up to 21 miles. The lens was manufactured in Birmingham, England, by Chance Brothers. At the time the tower was built, dwellings for the head keeper and both assistant keepers, barns, and oil houses were put into place. A small one-room schoolhouse was built for the three keepers and their families at the station.

1776.
Heceta Head from
Oregon Coast Highway

U. S. Light, Heceta Head, Oregon Coast.

ADDITIONAL VIEWS OF HECETA HEAD LIGHT. Around 1895, an area of rocks near the tower was removed to make the view more open from the north, having been made worse when a landslide brought rubble and rocks too close to the tower. Electricity came to the light station in 1934. After the electricity arrived, the workload was somewhat lessened, and the need for a second assistant was eliminated. By 1940, the single dwelling was demolished, and only the duplex dwelling was left. During World War II, the US Coast Guard used the Heceta Light Station as part of its coastal patrol. The light became automated in 1963. Now, the keeper's dwelling is used as a bed-and-breakfast.

16778-Heceta Head Light House -Oregon Coast

Umpqua Light House.

THE WINCHESTER BAY LIGHT. After a false start early on in 1853, the Umpqua River Lighthouse was built at the mouth of the Umpqua River near Winchester Bay in 1857 in the Oregon Territory. A 92-foot tower rose from the center of the gable roof of the Cape Cod–style keeper's house. When the area was chosen, the flooding that would occur was not noticed, and soon, the foundation gave way and made the structure unsound. With seasonal flooding in the area and the erosion of the sandy embankment, the longevity of the light was in certain question by 1864, when the decision was made by the tower collapse.

948 UMPQUA LIGHT HOUSE, OREGON COAST HIGHWAY

PHOTO BY WESLEY ANDREWS   7A-H3958

Umpqua Bay Light House, Oregon Coast

UMPQUA RIVER LIGHTHOUSE, WINCHESTER BAY. It took nearly 20 years before a new Umpqua River Lighthouse was started. When a new site for the light was chosen, it sat farther inland on a headland 100 feet above the river. It was not until 1893 that the keepers' dwelling, a duplex dwelling for the two assistant keepers, two oil houses, a cistern, and a barn were completed. The tower, built of brick with a cement plaster covering, was 65 feet tall, with a first-order Fresnel lens. The new light used a clocklike mechanism for the rotation of the lens. In 1934, electricity came to the light station with the help of a generator. (Below, courtesy of the US Coast Guard.)

ANOTHER VIEW OF UMPQUA RIVER LIGHTHOUSE. When the light was automated in 1966, it was then active 24 hours a day. At the same time, the outbuildings were demolished and removed from the site. A temporary rotating beacon was used at the tower when the chariot wheel became unusable after 89 years of use. The lens was put back into operation in 1985 after the community outrage changed the thinking of the US Coast Guard. In 2012, the Coast Guard turned over ownership of the Umpqua River Light to Douglas County, which gave it control of the operation and maintenance of the light. The first-order Fresnel lens is still an active aid for the maritime navigation of the river site.

Four

CALIFORNIA

82 Old Point Loma Light House .. San Diego, Calif.

THE FIRST POINT LOMA LIGHTHOUSE. Old Point Loma was one of eight lighthouses on the western coastline that were built in a similar Cape Cod style. It is located on the Point Loma Peninsula at the entrance to San Diego Bay, a narrow area of land on the west side of the harbor. In 1850, just after California had become a state and appropriations were made, construction of the light was started.

OLD POINT LOMA LIGHTHOUSE, SAN DIEGO. The one-and-a-half-story Cape Cod lighthouse had a spiral staircase in the middle of the building that led to the tower and lantern room constructed on the top of the dwelling. As with many of the lighthouse construction projects, getting supplies to the area was usually problematic; a road was needed to get the materials from the harbor. The lighthouse was constructed from brick and sandstone. The tower would hold a third-order Fresnel lens, with a visibility of 26 miles. With the finishing of the dwelling and tower, an additional supply structure was built. At first, the keeper and assistant shared the four-room dwelling until 1875, when the storeroom was made into an assistant keeper's quarters after a barn was added to the station.

Approach to Old Spanish Light... End of Point Loma, Calif. #115

ADDITIONAL VIEWS OF OLD POINT LOMA LIGHTHOUSE. Due to erosion caused by the weather, a coat of cement was used on the sides of the tower most exposed; eventually, it was used on the entire dwelling. Because of the height of the light and the foggy weather, the light was often not seen well enough. In 1891, the Port Loma Light was extinguished after the New Port Loma Light was lit from a metal tower. The light soon fell into disrepair, from neglect and vandals. By the 1980s, the light was refurbished and became part of the National Park Service. The year 2004 saw a few of the original structures rebuilt to offer a better visual for visitors as to how the keepers, assistants, and their families might have lived while tending the lighthouse.

old Spanish Lighthouse Point Loma Calif #351

TABLE BLUFF LIGHTHOUSE, TABLE BLUFF. A lighthouse was constructed in 1892 on the 165-foot-high Table Bluff in the Italianate Victorian style with the tower attached. It housed a fourth-order Fresnel lens. Added at the same time were a duplex keepers' house, a fog signal building, and supply structures. The station became electrified in 1935. After World War II, the US Coast Guard dismantled the dwelling, leaving only the tower standing. The light was deactivated in 1971.

SAN LUIS OBISPO LIGHTHOUSE, POINT SAN LUIS. In 1890, a Victorian-style lighthouse and keeper's cottage was constructed as a one-and-a-half-story dwelling with a square framed tower and fourth-order lens. It was placed in the southwestern corner. Additional housing in a one-and-a-half-story double keeper's dwelling, along with fog signal buildings and oil houses, was added. In 1969, the Fresnel lens was deactivated with full automation in place by 1974.

POINT VINCENTE LIGHTHOUSE, RANCHO PALOS VERDES. Located between Long Beach and Santa Monica, the Palos Verde Peninsula is where, in 1926, on the edge of a 130-foot cliff, three keepers' dwellings, built of wood and stucco with tile roofs, and a fog signal structure were constructed. A 67-foot tower made of reinforced concrete housed a third-order Fresnel lens with a visibility of 24 miles. World War II brought a dimming of the light, so as to not help the Japanese submarines. The light was automated in 1971 but housed US Coast Guard personnel for many years.

St. George Reef Lighthouse, Point St. George. Built from 1881 to 1890 on the North West Seal Rock, a formation of exposed and covered ledges, the lighthouse sits about six miles off the coast near Crescent City. The first step was using explosives to create a flat surface for building the foundation with concrete and granite blocks. Three hundred feet in diameter and 70 feet above the waterline, the tower went on to be the most expensive lighthouse ever built for that time. Its spiral staircase was used to access the lantern room and the first-order Fresnel lens. Five keepers had duty at the light for three months and then two months off to spend with families. In 1988, the St. George Reef Lighthouse Preservation Society was formed to restore the lighthouse. Now it is neither abandoned nor forgotten.

POINT CABRILLO LIGHTHOUSE, CASPER. As far back as 1873, the Point Cabrillo site was surveyed as a potential site for a light, but it was not until 1909 that the government purchased 30 acres on the point. The 47-foot octagonal tower was attached to the end of the one-and-a-half-story fog signal building. A third-order Fresnel lens was housed in the lantern room. Three two-story keepers' dwellings were constructed, with the middle building being the largest and used for the head keeper. By 1935, electricity came to the light station. Over the years, the erosion of the bluffs has made the point almost an island. In 1995, a restoration project was started at the station, which brought the blacksmith shop, keepers' dwellings, and oil house up to date. In 2006, the head keeper's dwelling was opened up as an inn.

GUARDIAN OF THE PACIFIC
PT. CABRILLO CALIF.

POINT PINOS LIGHTHOUSE, PACIFIC GROVE. First lit in 1855 to oversee the dangerous southern entrance to Monterey Bay, Point Pinos went on to become the oldest continuously operating lighthouse on the Pacific coast. It was built as a one-and-a-half-story stone keeper's dwelling, with a center situate tower rising from the roof. The lantern room saw the addition of a third-order Fresnel lens. In 1880, a porch was added to the east side of the dwelling, used to store supplies. In April 1906, Point Pinos Lighthouse was involved in an earthquake that gave the great light a massive shake, causing extensive damage.

95—Point Pinos Light House, Pacific Grove, California

PHOTO BY ROBERT A. PARKER

1771 Point Pinos Lighthouse, Pacific Grove California

ADDITIONAL VIEWS OF POINT PINOS LIGHTHOUSE. The earthquake made the removal of the lens and lantern room necessary, and five feet of the brick tower was taken down and rebuilt with reinforced concrete. It was not until 1925 that a fog signal was added to the station. Point Pinos was automated in 1975, when a battery-operated backup strobe light was installed outside of the tower, enabling the main light to be turned on permanently. The City of Pacific Grove took the license of the light and opened it as part of the Pacific Grove Natural History Museum. In 2006, the US Coast Guard transferred ownership of the light to the City of Pacific Grove.

Hueneme Light House, Hueneme, Cal.

POINT HUENEME LIGHTHOUSE, PORT HUENEME. When it was planned to place a lighthouse near Point Hueneme, there was indecision about whether Anacapa Island or the point would work better. The island was 12 miles from the point and 250 feet above sea level and rocky; it did not have the wood and water needed to support a lighthouse or its outbuildings. It is at the southern entrance to the Santa Barbara channel, where even though the low-lying ground, lagoons, and drifting sands made building there difficult, that the lighthouse was situated in 1873. The light was built in what was called a Craftsman style with Swiss and Elizabethan influences as a two-story structure with a square tower holding the fourth-order Fresnel lens in the lantern room, which extended from the pitched roofline.

The Light House, Hueneme, Cal.

LIGHT HOUSE AT HUENEME BEACH

HUENEME WHARF AND BEACH

THE FINEST BEACH ON PACIFIC COAST, NEAR OXNARD, CAL.

ADDITIONAL VIEWS OF POINT HUENEME LIGHTHOUSE. The dwellings contained 10 rooms with four fireplaces. The first floor was used by the head keeper and his family, and the assistant keeper, when needed, used the second floor. The same style of light was used for Point Fermin. In 1939, the lens and lantern room were removed and saved for the new light to be built. The lighthouse was sold at auction to be used as a yacht club, moved across the harbor but never finished, and then was torn down after years of neglect. By late 1940, a new Art Deco–style lighthouse with a 48-foot concrete tower and fog signal building was finished. Separate keeper dwellings were built nearby.

Piedras Blancas Lighthouse, California
Light, White, Fixed, varied by a White Flash every 15 seconds, visible 19¼ miles.
Fog Signal is a Compressed-Air Whistle.

PIEDRAS BLANCAS LIGHTHOUSE, SAN SIMEON. In California, most of the lighthouses did not need to be built to great heights because of the cliffs and bluffs they were placed on. With no high bluffs in this area in 1875, the need for a light at Point Piedras Blancas became apparent, and a 100-foot-tall conical-shaped brick tower was built. Its lantern room held a first-order Fresnel lens with a visibility of 21 miles. The area was known for its lumber and farm produce, and shipping these products along the coast was a hazard without the light from Point Piedras Blancas. Soon, a two-story Victorian residence was built with 12 rooms for the families of the keeper and the assistants. By 1903, funds were established to build a fog signal structure and a second residence for an additional keeper to help with the running of the station.

ADDITIONAL VIEWS OF PIEDRAS BLANCAS LIGHTHOUSE. A telephone system was set up between the light tower, fog station, and the residences because of the distance between them when built. In 1948, a 4.6 magnitude earthquake hit the station six miles from the epicenter just offshore. With the damage it caused to the tower, the lantern room, lens, railing, and top section of the tower were removed. In place, a rotating aero beacon was placed atop the now enclosed remaining portion of the tower. After leaving the lens on the pad for 40 years, a restoration effort was put into place in 1990. In 1960, the old Victorian triplex was demolished, and ranch-style homes were put in place to house the US Coast Guard. When the light was automated in 1975, the Coast Guard was removed. In 2012, protective paint was used on the tower.

Alcatraz Lighthouse, San Francisco Bay, Cal., U.S.A.
Light, Flashing White, visible 19 miles.

ALCATRAZ ISLAND LIGHTHOUSE, SAN FRANCISCO BAY. In 1854, Alcatraz became one of seven lights to be constructed along the Pacific coast using the same plans for a one-and-a-half-story schoolhouse-type building with a tower rising from the pitched roof. Stairs were used to get to the second floor and the lantern room. A third-order Fresnel lens was used to light the tower. There was a head keeper and an assistant. It was during the Civil War that Alcatraz was first used as a prison. With the completion of the lighthouse, the island was soon used as a military base. Due to the 1906 earthquake in San Francisco and the dwelling's chimney falling, a crack in the tower brought concern.

ALCATRAZ ISLAND, SAN FRANCISCO BAY, UNITED STATES MILITARY PRISON IS LOCATED HERE.

ALCATRAZ ISLAND - SAN FRANCISCO BAY

ADDITIONAL VIEWS OF ALCATRAZ ISLAND LIGHTHOUSE. In 1909, a new reinforced concrete cell house was built with 600 cells. A taller light was needed, and a 90-foot tower was built using the original fourth-order lens, and at the base of the tower, two double-story wings were added for the use of the keeper and his assistants for housing. Having been used as a military prison until 1933, Alcatraz was transferred to the US Justice Department to be used as a penitentiary for federal prisoners. Many prison guards and their families lived on what was now called "the Rock." The prison closed as a penitentiary in 1963. After a Native American occupation of the island in 1970, some damage occurred to the housing and tower. In 1971, the light was once again relit.

Carquinez Strait Lighthouse. California.

CARQUINEZ STRAIT LIGHT, VALLEJO. In 1907, in the Carquinez Strait, wooden piles were placed deep into the muddy bottom of the strait with a steam pile driver to build a long pier that extended out into the water from the shore. Next, a dock was built with a platform to construct a large 28-room, two-and-a-half-story structure with an attached three-story tower built into the southwest corner. This housed three keepers and their families. In 1951, the light was replaced with a smaller beacon after the pier was extended. The large lightkeeper's residence was offered for sale in 1955 and included the Fresnel lens. Problems occurred while trying to move the residence, including vandals gaining entrance and smashing the lens. Ultimately, the residence became known as the Lighthouse Inn. (Below, courtesy of Project Gutenberg's *Lightships and Lighthouses*.)

FARALLON ISLAND LIGHTHOUSE, FARALLON ISLAND. The lighthouse was constructed as a 41-foot tapered cylindrical brick and stone tower in 1855 to warn ships approaching San Francisco from the west away from the rocky islands. The lights tower holds a first-order Fresnel lens. In 1878, and again in 1880, two identical Victorian-style duplexes were built on the island to be used as residences for the head keeper and his assistants' families. The lighthouse was automated in 1972.

HUMBOLDT HARBOR LIGHTHOUSE, HUMBOLDT BAY. In 1856, a one-and-a-half-story building with a central tower and a lantern room housing a fourth-order Fresnel lens sat at the north end of Humboldt Harbor on a spit near the harbor entrance. Damage was done to the lighthouse in the earthquakes of 1877 and 1882 as well as a cyclone in 1885. With that, the lighthouse was officially decommissioned in 1892. Left to decay, the central tower collapsed in 1933, and only some foundation walls survive today.

Crescent City Light House,
Crescent City, Cal.
1052-MAT-RAX

BATTERY POINT LIGHTHOUSE, CRESCENT CITY. In 1856, Battery Point became home to a newly built Cape Cod–style one-and-a-half-story residence with a central tower protruding from the roof of the structure. The lantern room held a fourth-order Fresnel lens. Built on an islet, it was connected to Battery Point by an isthmus, which can be seen at low tide. Being battered by the water and weather was a normal occurrence for the light. Although the color of the lighthouse changed over the years, in 1887 it was painted white along with the tower, and that was to remain its daymark.

ADDITIONAL VIEWS OF BATTERY POINT LIGHTHOUSE. In 1953, the light became automated. In 1964, the worst tsunami to hit the West Coast, due to an earthquake that struck Alaska near Prince William Sound, sent waves upwards of 20 feet high, which hit the lighthouse. The lighthouse survived the water intact. In 1982, the light became a private aid for navigation and continued to be lit. Today, caretakers live in the lighthouse and give tours when the tide is low and access is available.

LOS ANGELES HARBOR LIGHTHOUSE, LOS ANGELES. The San Pedro Breakwater in Los Angeles Harbor is where one will find the light once known as Angels Gate Light. In 1913, a structural steel frame was erected on the pierhead, and an octagonal structure was built and encased in steel plates with a cylindrical tower constructed in concrete. It was styled with 12 pilaster columns that were painted black to make its daymark more visible against the white tower. A fourth-order Fresnel lens had a visibility of 14 miles. A 6.4 magnitude earthquake hit the area in 1933, but the tower sustained the tremors. In 1966, a three-foot-long seal named Charlie by the keepers seemed to move in and kept them company for a while. The light was automated in 1975. A modern beacon was installed after the removal of the Fresnel lens in 1987.

1175 – Ballast Point, Entrance to San Diego Bay, California.

BALLAST POINT LIGHTHOUSE, POINT LOMA. Because of fog in the area, when many of the other lighthouses were built on bluffs, the Ballast Point Lighthouse was constructed at sea level in 1890 and used to make the waterways safer for navigation into San Diego Bay. Ballast Point is a small peninsula extending from Point Loma at the entrance to the channel leading into the harbor at San Diego. Two buildings to be used as keepers' quarters were erected with a two-story square wooden tower attached to one of the houses, which held a lantern room and a boathouse. By 1960, the dwellings were torn down, leaving the wood tower standing free. By 1961, an offshore light was established, and the old tower was placed on a flatbed and hauled away to a private residence.

Ballast Point Light House
from Point Loma, Calif. 81

Light House, Santa Cruz, Cal.

SANTA CRUZ LIGHTHOUSE, SANTA CRUZ. Sitting on the western side of Monterey Bay at Point Santa Cruz, the lighthouse was built in 1869 to copy the Ediz Hook Lighthouse in Washington. In what could be called a schoolhouse design, the light tower protruded from the roof of the one-and-a-half-story house. It had a fifth-order Fresnel lens in the octagonal-shaped lantern room. In 1879, concerned that the lighthouse could collapse, it was moved 300 feet north of its first location. The light was deactivated in 1941, and the original building was auctioned off for private use. Due to the untimely death of a young man surfing in 1965, his parents donated money to build a new lighthouse in the area he loved, and it became the Mark Abbott Memorial Lighthouse and Santa Cruz Surfing Museum, with Abbott's ashes buried at the base of the new tower.

POINT SUR LIGHTHOUSE, POINT SUR STATE PARK. Point Sur is a large 361-foot-tall rock with lowland connecting the rock to the mainland. There are times when water has surrounded the rock, cutting it off from the mainland. In 1889, a three-story triplex was constructed to house three keepers and their families, with another building used for a fourth keeper. Fencing was arranged around the dwellings for the safety of the children. A first-order Fresnel lens was housed in the lantern room. Supplies were brought out to the light by tender every four months. The point was used as a lookout during World War II. By 1972, the lighthouse was automated, and after the US Coast Guard left the site that year, the buildings were boarded up for protection. Preservation will continue making this one of the most complete light stations in California.

POINT CONCEPTION LIGHTHOUSE, POINT CONCEPTION. At the west entrance of the Santa Barbara Channel is Point Conception, where in 1856 a one-story, 38-by-20-foot, Cape Cod–style dwelling with a wooden tower protruding from the center of the roofline was built high on the sandstone cliffs. A new light in the 1880s needed to be considered because of low fog in the area. When a new light was built lower on the cliffs, it made the fog less likely to inhibit the beam of the light. A fourth-order Fresnel lens was placed on the new tower in 1882, giving the area a 20-mile visibility.

ADDITIONAL VIEWS OF POINT CONCEPTION LIGHTHOUSE. A new duplex dwelling for lightkeepers was built in 1905. A reinforced dwelling replaced the original lighthouse in 1911. In 1917, the steam whistles were replaced with a new diaphone fog signal. Electricity came to Point Conception in 1948, which made it the last lighthouse to become electrified on the Pacific coast. The light station became automated in 1973. Although the Fresnel lens was still working in 1999, the expense of repairs to the lens to keep it revolving made it necessary to use a modern beacon as the lamp. Today, the lighthouse is part of a private ranch.

LIGHT HOUSE, POINT CONCEPCION CAL.

Point Conception Lighthouse, California.
Light White Flashing, visible 17 miles.

91

Light House, Golden Gate, San Francisco, California

MILE ROCKS LIGHTHOUSE, LANDS END, SAN FRANCISCO. Mile Rocks Lighthouse, built in 1906, got its name from its location, which was one mile south of the main shipping line into the San Francisco Bay. It took a tragic shipping accident with great loss of life for the engineers to find a way to build the Mile Rocks Light. A 35-foot-high concrete and steel lower portion was constructed as a base. A three-tiered steel tower was added, including the lantern room with a third-order Fresnel lens. The different levels were used for the keepers to live and have room for storage. By 1966, the US Coast Guard decided to automate the light and then removed the top two tiers of the tower and converted it into a helicopter landing pad. The base now is painted in orange and white stripes.

Mile Rock Light House, Golden Gate Strait, San Francisco, California

MARE ISLAND LIGHTHOUSE, VALLEJO. At the entrance to the Carquinez Strait is Pablo Bay, and on the southern end of Mare Island in 1873, a lighthouse was built using the same design style as her five other sister lights: Point Fermin, East Brother, Hereford Light, Point Hueneme, and Point Adams, all along the Pacific coast. A keeper's dwelling, a 76-foot tower, a fog signal, a boat landing, and a tramway to receive supplies from the beach were put in place. The fourth-order lens was damaged during the earthquake in 1906, along with other structural damage. With the opening of the Carquinez Strait Lighthouse in 1909, this lighthouse was built in a better location; therefore, Mare Island Light was deactivated in 1917 and demolished in 1930.

POINT BONITA LIGHTHOUSE, SAN FRANCISCO BAY. The first light at Point Bonita was built in 1855. It was a 56-foot brick tower housing a second-order Fresnel lens and sat 300 feet above sea level. The need for the light to be moved came at the realization that with the fog at lower levels, the light could not be seen. In 1877, the light was moved to the southwestern tip of Point Bonita, a lower location at only 124 feet above sea level, and because of the dense rock, a 118-foot-long tunnel was carved through the hard rock to access the site.

ADDITIONAL VIEWS OF POINT BONITA LIGHTHOUSE. In 1906, Point Bonita was another light station that sustained damage from the earthquake. With damage to the assistant keepers' dwellings, it was necessary to construct new double buildings in 1908. One keeper built harnesses to tether his children whenever they played outside; a good foresight, as his daughter was found dangling over the cliff in her harness one day. The lighthouse could be reached by foot until erosion made a gap in the trail. By 1954, a suspension bridge, looking very much like the Golden Gate Bridge, was built to allow access to and from the lighthouse. The US Coast Guard continues to maintain the light and fog signal today. (Above, courtesy of the *Los Angeles Times*; below, courtesy of the US Coast Guard.)

POINT REYES LIGHTHOUSE

POINT REYS LIGHTHOUSE, GULF OF FARALLONES. In 1870, after finally acquiring the land that Point Reyes needed for a light at this position, two flat areas were carved out of the rocky cliffs at about 100 feet above the sea for the fog signal building, and another area was carved out 150 feet higher for the light tower. A wooden stairway was needed to reach the tower, which required 300 steps to be built into the cliff and an additional 338 steps to reach the fog signal building below. The lighthouse tower is a 37-foot, 16-sided structure forged out of iron plating, with a first-order Fresnel lens housed in the lantern room. By 1885, a two-story dwelling was built for the keepers at the top of the bluff, along with additional cottages.

ADDITIONAL VIEWS OF POINT REYS LIGHTHOUSE. For a number of years, there were concerns that the fog signal was inefficient for maritime traffic. By 1915, an air diaphone was installed, which seemed to solve the problem, allowing shipmates to hear the signal many miles out to sea. Because of the continued fog and wind, with records showing the point was the windiest and foggiest light on the Pacific coast, the Point Reyes assignments were not always enjoyed by the keepers. The light was electrified in 1938. The year 1939 brought much-needed concrete steps to the light station. By 1960, a four-plex building was erected with both two- and three-bedroom units for the keeper and three assistants. The station was automated in 1975. The National Park Service opened the light for tours in 1977.

TRINIDAD LIGHT HOUSE, California Photo. A. W. Ericson, Arcata, Cal.

TRINIDAD HEAD LIGHTHOUSE, TRINIDAD.
On the bluffs overlooking the bay, Trinidad is the oldest town on the Northern California coast, with Trinidad Head, a large protrusion rising 380 feet up, a part of the bluff. In 1881, a short, square brick tower with its daymark painted white was built with a fourth-order Fresnel lens at 196 feet above the sea. A Victorian residence for a keeper and a barn were part of the original station. The year 1898 brought a 4,000-pound fog bell to the site, but after a couple of years, the weight cables snapped, and the weights fell down the cliff into the sea. A second keeper was added to the station around this time.

ADDITIONAL VIEWS OF TRINIDAD HEAD LIGHTHOUSE. Electricity came to the bluff in 1942. Back in 1953, a visitor, Ralph Hayes, came to enjoy the sights at Trinidad Head Lighthouse and commemorated his trip with a photographic image. The original keeper's residence was torn down in the late 1960s, and in its place, the US Coast Guard built a triplex dwelling to house its personnel. The year 1974 saw automation come to the station, but it would be 2000 before all the Coast Guard presence was removed. The Bureau of Land Management now manages the site.

Light House on Trinidad Head. Redwood Hwy.

The Light House near Santa Barbara, Cal.

SANTA BARBARA LIGHTHOUSE, SANTA BARBARA. When it was realized a lighthouse was needed in the Santa Barbara area, it was decided that both a harbor light and a seacoast light would work best. In late 1856, as with many of the other lights along the Pacific coast, a building with a tower rising in the center of the roofline took its place. The tower had a fourth-order Fresnel lens in the lantern room. After nine years, the first lightkeeper became tired of the duties of the light and retired. His wife, Julia Williams, became the head keeper. Her work was so good that she was made official in 1865 and kept that position until 1905 when, due to an accident at 81 years, she was relieved. Julia also raised five children at the light.

The Lighthouse and Mrs. Williams, Santa Barbara, Cal. Oldest Woman Lighthouse Tender in the U. S.

"The Lighthouse Lady"
Julia Williams, 1865-1905
at Santa Barbara Light, California

ADDITIONAL VIEWS OF SANTA BARBARA LIGHTHOUSE. In June 1925, Santa Barbara was shaken by a severe earthquake. At 6:45 in the morning, the tower and lantern room came crashing down upon the walls, completely flattening the dwelling and also shattering the Fresnel lens, making the site a total loss. Soon, a 24-foot enclosed steel tower was erected, and that beacon was used from 1935 until 1977. A current light is maintained by the US Coast Guard inside a fenced compound on a nearby bluff.

LIGHT-HOUSE TOWER 35.
STA. BARBARA EARTH QUAKE.
6-29-25

YERBA BUENA LIGHT STATION (GOAT ISLAND), SAN FRANCISCO, CALIFORNIA

YERBA BUENA LIGHTHOUSE, YERBA BUENA ISLAND. Located between San Francisco and Oakland, the small island saw, in 1875, a 25-foot octagonal Victorian-style tower built of wood placed on the southwest end of Yerba Buena Island. A fifth-order Fresnel lens from the old Yaquina Bay Lighthouse was housed in the lantern room. Farther up the hill from the tower, a two-story keeper's residence was also built. Soon, the cliff face in front of the light station was painted white to add a daymark to make its presence known. In 1897, the keeper's house was enlarged, and during that summer, a fourth-order lens was exchanged for the fifth-order lens that had originally been used.

Light-house on Yerba Buena (Goat) Island.

1706 – Light House, Yerba Buena Island, San Francisco Bay, California.

ADDITIONAL VIEWS OF YERBA BUENA LIGHTHOUSE. In 1909, the assistant keeper noticed a crackling noise and soon realized that the roof of the building he was sitting in was on fire. At the same time, a US Navy tug noticed the fire and set off the alarm, bringing help from the naval training center. The fire was extinguished but with damage to the roof and upper floors. The island's name was officially changed in 1912 to Goat Island, with the people of the area showing such great displeasure at the change that by 1931, the old Spanish name was restored to the island. During World War II, the Navy used the island station and continued to do so until 1993. It is operational and used today.

Point Loma Lighthouse, San Diego, Cal.

NEW POINT LOMA LIGHTHOUSE, SAN DIEGO. In 1891, a lighthouse was built on the southernmost tip of the Point Loma Peninsula in San Diego. The lower elevation made it an ideal spot to take the place of the original Point Loma Lighthouse, which was a constant source of concern because it was quite often covered in fog. Two Victorian cottages for the keeper and assistant were built along with a tubular lighthouse. Along with the tower, a spiral staircase, a central tube, and supporting framework, a two-story lantern room was added to complete the 75 pyramidal tower. The original Fresnel lens ordered for the tower arrived, but it was too large for the lantern room; finally, a third-order lens was acquired for the lantern room.

Point Loma Light House, San Diego, Cal.

J. C. Packard, San Diego, Cal.

104

ADDITIONAL VIEWS OF NEW POINT LOMA LIGHTHOUSE. In 1894, the brown color of the tower was changed to white as its daymark. The year 1912 saw a fog signal become part of the light station in the way of a square building with a double-hipped roofline that was constructed just north of the tower, where it housed a compressed-air fog signal. During World War II, the light station, in order to make it less visible, was painted a drab olive color, and a blackout order was imposed on the station. The lighthouse was automated in 1973. In 1993, due the constant movement of the Fresnel lens rotation 24 hours a day, it came to a stop from the rust and warping. Placed in canvas, the antique lens was replaced, and a beacon was used in its place. In 2002, the lens was dismantled and put into storage.

East Brother Island Lights Cal.

East Brother Lighthouse, San Pablo Bay. In 1874, a lighthouse was built in the Victorian style, with a three-story tower housing a fourth-order Fresnel lens attached to the two-story dwelling. An assistant keeper's dwelling was added, along with an equipment building, cistern, and water tank for catching rainwater. Shortly after, a fog signal was also added to the station. Electricity came to the station in 1934, and during that time, a fifth-order lens was switched to the fourth-order lens that had been in use. The US Coast Guard took over the responsibility of the lighthouse in 1939. With the station becoming automated in the 1960s to save the Coast Guard funds, the possibility of demolishing the station was entertained. The Contra Costa Shoreline Parks Committee started an effort to save the station. It is now used as a bed-and-breakfast.

OAKLAND HARBOR LIGHTHOUSE, EMBARCADERO COVE. In 1890, at the entrance to Oakland Harbor, 11 wooden pilings were driven into the bay, and a rectangular two-story keeper's dwelling was built off the end of the northern pier. The lantern room housed a fifth-order Fresnel lens. In 1897, an additional eight piles were driven into the bay to support a two-room addition on the north side of the lighthouse. Concrete a foot thick was poured around the pilings because shipworm had weakened the older piles by 1899. By 1902, the piles deteriorated to the point a new lighthouse was built with concrete pilings. A square two-story structure with steel decking was constructed next. This second lighthouse was sold in 1966 to a private owner who opened a restaurant in 1984 at Embarcadero Cove in Oakland.

PIGEON POINT LIGHTHOUSE, PIGEON POINT. The first to be built on the point was the Victorian-style four-plex and a fog signal in 1871. Then a 115-foot brick tower was built but with numerous delays, from difficulty with the spiral staircase to getting the first-order Fresnel lens assembled in the lantern room. Both Pigeon Point Light and Port Arena Light share the title of being the tallest lighthouse towers in California. In 1878, one of the children of a keeper fell over the bluff into the sea, so safety was causing anxious times for the families stationed there. By 1906, there were four keepers and their families living at the point, and additional living quarters were needed. In 1960, the original four-plex was demolished to be replaced by four ranch-style dwellings.

Pigeon Pt. Light House, Pescadero, Cal.

1751. Pigeon Point Light-House, Coast of California.

ADDITIONAL VIEWS OF PIGEON POINT LIGHTHOUSE. The name for the point came about in 1853 when a ship named the *Carrier Pigeon* ran aground at the point, and from that time, the land closest to where the ship had wrecked was called Pigeon Point. The station was automated in 1974 after a rotating beacon was placed in the balcony of the lantern room when the Fresnel lens was deactivated. The tower was closed to the public after pieces of the brick and iron cornice fell to the ground in 2001. The lighthouse was transferred to the State of California in 2005 to help with restoration and the reopening of the light to the public. In 2011, the Fresnel lens was removed from the lantern room and is now displayed in the fog signal building.

POINT ARGUELLO LIGHTHOUSE, SANTA BARBARA CHANNEL. The Santa Barbara Channel lies between Point Arguello and Point Conception, at a very dangerous place for navigation. It took until 1899 for funding to come across for the light to be built, 12 miles northwest of Point Conception, to ease traffic into the channel. A one-story rectangular fog building had a tower extending from the pitched roof at the western end with a circular lantern room that housed a fourth-order Fresnel lens. Standing apart from the lighthouse, two buildings, a single-family residence, and a two-story duplex for the keepers were erected. (Below, courtesy of the US Coast Guard Collection.)

ADDITIONAL VIEWS OF POINT ARGUELLO LIGHTHOUSE. A blacksmith shop, oil house, and barn were added to the station. The light tower attached to the fog signal building was replaced in 1911 by a stand-alone tower, just adjacent to the structure. In 1934, the lighthouse was replaced by a pair of 36-inch revolving aero beacons mounted on steel skeleton towers. With the US Coast Guard assuming responsibility for the light in 1939, the keepers' housing was made into barracks, and more ranch-style housing was built. Those original buildings were torn down in 1967. Now, Point Arguello is part of Vandenberg Air Force Base and is not open to the public. (Below, courtesy of the Library of Congress.)

POINT ARENA LIGHT HOUSE, BUILT 1908. HEIGHT 110 FT.

POINT ARENA LIGHTHOUSE, MENDOCINO COUNTY. Punta Barro de Arena, another name for Sand Bar Point, later became Point Arena, a narrow peninsular two miles north of the town of Point Arena. The first lighthouse built in 1870 was constructed of brick and mortar and stood 100 feet tall with a first-order Fresnel lens housed in the lantern room. A large two-and-a-half-story dwelling, also built of brick like the tower, was constructed for the four keepers and their families. In the years 1880, 1887, and 1898, the lighthouse experienced earthquakes that created massive tremors. In 1906, the San Francisco earthquake hit the light station, where the lighthouse and the keeper's residence were damaged to the point of needing to be demolished. The material from that demolished tower and dwelling was hauled over the cliffs into the sea.

East of Tower
Pt Arena Light

ANOTHER VIEW OF POINT ARENA LIGHTHOUSE. In 1908, a new earthquake-proof lighthouse made with reinforced concrete was constructed. With the tower completed, a buttress was built around the base of the tower for extra support, where there was also space for a workroom. The new tower at 115 feet also had a first-order Fresnel lens housed in this lantern room. For the keepers and their families, four single dwellings were built in a row to the south of the new tower. The daymark of the light had the gallery around the lantern room painted black, but after the US Coast Guard took possession in 1939, the daymark on the tower became totally white. The year 1960 had four new ranch-style keepers' bungalows built with the others being demolished. The station was automated in 1977. Renovations from 2008 to 2010 allowed for people to once again visit the lighthouse.

Pt. Fermin Lighthouse, San Pedro, Cal

POINT FERMIN LIGHTHOUSE, SAN PEDRO.
Point Fermin overlooks the harbor of San Pedro, where in 1874 construction started on the bluff with the redwood coming from the forest of California. Because of multiple owners at the time, condemnation proceedings needed to take place to acquire the land that the lighthouse needed at the point. There were a number of outbuildings constructed along with two cisterns to complete the station. The dwelling was a two-story Victorian with the two-story tower protruding from the pitched roofline. Its fourth-order Fresnel lens was housed in the lantern room.

ADDITIONAL VIEWS OF POINT FERMIN LIGHTHOUSE. As most of the lights on the West Coast were extinguished after Pearl Harbor in 1941, so was Point Fermin, to avoid aiding the Japanese submarines often not far offshore. The lantern room was removed, and the top of the tower was reconstructed in a boxlike enclosure for use as a lookout tower. When the war was over, a pole near the edge of the bluff with a light replaced the lighthouse. In 1972, thoughts of demolishing the lighthouse structure were discarded when it was added to the National Register of Historic Places. The lookout box was removed, and a new lantern room was built. In 2002, restoration took place in the way of painting, plumbing, and electrical work.

The Light House, Point Firmin, San Pedro, Cal.

POINT FERMIN LIGHTHOUSE
Built in 1876
Point Fermin Park, San Pedro, California   B 8254

THE ORNATE VICTORIANS. Point Fermin's sister stations—East Brother Island Light in Richmond, Mare Island Light in the Carquinez Strait, and Point Hueneme Light in Point Hueneme (all in California); Hereford Inlet Light in North Wood, New Jersey; and Point Adams Light in Washington State—were all built of the same ornate Victorian style. The original fourth-order Fresnel lens at Point Fermin was removed from the tower in 1942 and went missing for many decades. When restoration was being done in 2002, a tip while having a casual meal led to the ultimate finding of the original lens, where, within a short time, the lens was brought back to the lighthouse and displayed on the ground floor. It is now open to the public as the Point Fermin Lighthouse Historic Site and Museum.

Six

Hawaii

The Honolulu Light. Following discussions and ideas for many years, in 1869, Honolulu Harbor got its first lighthouse, with wooden pilings driven into the reef on a very small island in the harbor. Also built were a keeper's dwelling and a square, pyramidal light tower with a lantern room housing a fourth-order Fresnel lens with a visibility of nine miles. It served as a front-range light for the harbor. In 1906, the harbor saw a new vision.

Aloha Tower, Honolulu.

ALOHA TOWER (HONOLULU LIGHT), HONOLULU. In 1906, Hawaii became a territory of the United States, and the lighthouse fell under the purview of the US Lighthouse Board. Work then started on a new lighthouse for the entrance to the harbor. A rectangular one-and-a-half-storied structure had a keeper's quarters and a fourth-order Fresnel lens. By 1926, a modern freight and passenger terminal was being built at Piers 8, 9, and 10 in the harbor. A 12-story steel structure was soon started with the 11th floor having balconies on all four sides. Below the balconies, the word "ALOHA" was spelled out as a greeting for all newcomers to the island. The top floor held a beacon for the navigational use of shipping coming into the area. The tower had other features as well, and a clock face was added to each side.

5-683 Aloha Tower

ANOTHER VIEW OF ALOHA TOWER (HONOLULU LIGHT). When built, the tower was planned to contain offices for the harbormaster, pilots, and officials running the terminal. During World War II, the Aloha Tower received very little damage in the bombing of Pearl Harbor, but soon after, the tower was painted in camouflaged colors to make it less visible. The harbor light on the tower was turned off until after the war. In 1948, the building was returned to its original color. In 1975, a light was added on Pier 2, and the tower's service as a navigational aid came to a close. In 1981, a corporation was formed to develop the land around the tower with access to the waterfront. In 1994, the State of Hawaii renovated the tower with the help of a developer of the Aloha Tower Marketplace.

H - 271 Aloha Tower, Honolulu

Aloha Tower, Honolulu

MAKAPU'U LIGHTHOUSE, OAHU. Makapu'u Point is at the southernmost point of Oahu, where the harbor of Honolulu and all those entering the harbor set eyes on it. In 1909, a design for a short tower was used so that it would keep the light as low as possible because the point is 647 feet above the ocean. The point, being made of blue lava rock, had to be blasted flat to build the three keepers' dwellings and a road connecting the station to the roadway. The 35-foot concrete tower would house a first-order hyper-radiant lens; this lens would be the only lens of this size in the United States. The US Coast Guard automated the light in 1974 and monitored the light from Honolulu. In 2001, land around Makapu'u Point was acquired to keep the area free from development.

KILAUEA POINT LIGHTHOUSE, KALIHIWAI.
Kilauea Point was where, in 1913 on
a narrow, peninsular protruding from
the northern shore of Kauai, a 52-foot
reinforced concrete tower was constructed.
Iron was used for the spiral staircase and for
the lantern room housing the second-order
Fresnel lens. Three keepers' dwellings were
built using blue volcanic rock found near
the site. Each of the residences had a living
space, kitchen, bathroom, two bedrooms,
and a storeroom. Rainwater was collected
from the roofs into concrete cisterns. In
1974, the US Coast Guard automated the
lighthouse. Kilauea Point became part of the
Kilauea Point National Wildlife Refuge. By
2008, restoration began to secure the tower.

DIAMOND HEAD LIGHTHOUSE, HONOLULU. On the island of Oahu, mariners used Diamond Head as a landmark to the approach to Honolulu Harbor. The name came from the calcite crystals thought to be diamonds by the early sailors who came to the point. The first light, constructed in 1898, was a 57-foot concrete, square-shaped pyramidal tower with a circular balcony and lantern room. Its external staircase wrapped around a portion of the tower, and the light was painted white with a red dome for its daymark. By 1916, there was concern regarding the integrity of the tower due to cracks in the structure.

ADDITIONAL VIEWS OF DIAMOND HEAD LIGHTHOUSE. Construction began on a new 57-foot reinforced concrete tower next to the original one in 1917. Using scaffolding around the old tower, the lantern room was removed and, on a new metal framework, placed on the new tower. The new tower had an internal iron spiral staircase to the lantern room. In 1921, the first keeper's dwelling was constructed, and by 1924, the light became automated when electricity was brought to the light station. In 1939, the US Coast Guard was stationed at the lighthouse for the duration of World War II, and a radio station was housed in the keeper's residence. (Below, courtesy of the hitachiota collection.)

LAHAINA LIGHTHOUSE, LAHAINA. This light was built on a section of waterfront known as *keawaiki*, a narrow break in the coral reef. While proceeding lights had been built in previous years, it was not until the US Lighthouse Board assumed control that a more permanent light was installed. A 39-foot pyramid, wood-encased, concrete tower was constructed in 1905 to replace the previous wooden trestle tower. A metal ladder was attached to the side of the tower to access the lantern room. The US Coast Guard dedicated the present light in 1916.

BARBERS POINT LIGHTHOUSE, KAPOLEI.
On the southern tip of the island of Oahu, Kalaeloa is where one will find Barbers Point and the first 42-foot cylindrical concrete tower, with a white daymark. In 1933, a second 72-foot, reinforced concrete tower was built next to the original tower. The lantern room and lens were transferred from the original to the new tower. Since electricity had come to the station, the lantern room now used a 500-watt bulb. The year 1964 came with the tower becoming automated and no longer requiring lightkeepers. (Both, courtesy of the US Coast Guard.)

MOLOKA'I LIGHTHOUSE, KALAUPAPA. The north shore of Moloka'i has high cliffs that drop down to the ocean, but a peninsula protrudes from the area with the ocean on three sides and a sheer drop on the other. A 132-foot octagonal tower was constructed in 1906, with concrete stairs up to the fourth-floor landing; the remainder were made of cast iron. The lantern room housed a second-order Fresnel lens. Three one-and-a-half-story keepers' dwellings, with living quarters, a kitchen, and two bedrooms, were built out of concrete or volcanic rock, near the tower. The last lightkeeper left the station in 1966. It is now part of the Kalaupapa National Historic Park. (Courtesy of the US Coast Guard.)

BIBLIOGRAPHY

D'Entremont, Jeremy. *The Lighthouse Handbook: West Coast*. Kennebunkport, ME: Cider Mill Press Book Publishers, 2016.

lighthousefriends.com

Roberts, Bruce, and Cheryl Shelton-Roberts. *American Lighthouses: A Comprehensive Guide to Exploring Our National Coastal Treasures*. Lanham, MD: Roman & Littlefield Publishing Group, Inc., 2020.

Stander, Bella. California and Hawaii Lighthouses Illustrated Map and Guide. Rhinebeck, NY: Bella Terra Publishing, 2016.

———. *Northwest Lighthouses Illustrated Map and Guide: Oregon, Washington, and Alaska*. Rhinebeck, NY: Bella Terra Publishing, 2018.

www.cgaux.org

www.dhs.gov

www.loc.gov/pictures

www.uslhs.org, The Keepers Log, Winter 2002

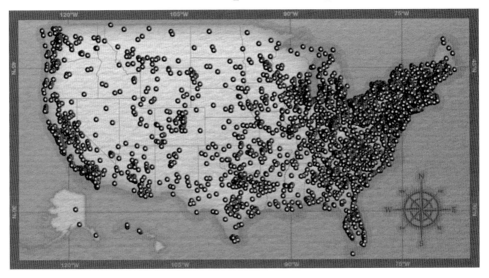